The Law

Of

Attraction

Ask, Believe, Receive

By: Richard A. McLeod

Table of Contents

Chapter 1:

Universal Truth of Attraction

Simply put, Attraction Mantra Secrets is the ability to use one's thoughts and intentions to attract things they want. The theory behind the Attraction Mantra Secrets is that we create our own realities. We are the magnet that attract our reality. It uses the power of mind to translate whatever is in our thoughts and materialize them into reality. This explains the significance of focusing on the positive things that you want to attract.

Attraction Mantra Secrets On the other hand, if you choose to focus on the negative doom and gloom you will remain under that cloud. Therefore, starve the negative thoughts by removing your attention.

By transforming your mindset to focus on what you want, rather than what you don't have, you will come to view the world in a different way. Each thought you have will bring you closer to your goal, rather than bringing you down and focusing you on what you might never have. Once you understand the power of your thought and direct this powerful tool in the direction of things that you desire, then you will discover that the action part of your life is the way you enjoy what you have created through your thoughts. The power of the lies in the fact that whatever you think about and believe will ultimately become the reality you experience.

Although the theory behind the Attraction Mantra Secrets is very simple, putting it into practice on a conscious level takes work. Negative and limiting belief systems are buried deep inside us. They are the ones which stop you from succeeding, achieving, and manifesting. Changing or ridding yourself of ideas and old habits that defeat you at every turn is possible. Are you up to the challenge? Start by learning how to activate the "Attraction Mantra Secrets ". The activation process involves three steps to eliminate limiting beliefs and attracting all your desires. Here are the 3 powerful tips to activate the Attraction Mantra Secrets:

1) Empty Your Mind

Meditate

Get a place that's quiet to meditate. Avoid noisy places where dogs are barking or individuals talking. This may distract you from focusing and too many distractions may prove too much to manage and you might stop meditating as soon as you begin. Get a comfortable, peaceful place with pleasant temperature to settle down. You don't want to meditate under the hot blazing sun or have all kinds of insects flying by, landing on you, biting you, and so forth. Initially these things may greatly distract you. Once you have settled down, all you need to do is to sit cross-legged, relaxed and have yourself meditate undisturbed up to an hour.

Breathe:

Observe your breath. There are a lot of things to observe... pace of taking a breath... the consistency of the tempo of breathing does it always remain the same as you sit? The smoothness of the breath or the abnormality of it. The depth or shallowness of breath... and, does it alter over time or is each breath a carbon copy of the last? Where do you sense the breath? Your nose? Your throat? Your mouth? Your lungs? Your tummy? Do you observe your diaphragm muscle beneath your ribs contracting and decompressing to enable you to breathe? Truly, only 2 things are required for excellent changes to happen inside your brain... a focus on the breath and mindfulness during the day when not meditating. Begin your common sitting session with getting comfy in your sitting posture and watch all the matters going on with your body and brain... attempt to unwind and calm the brain down...Observe the physical sensations happening... Observe the breath. Watch the breath.

Exercise:

Regardless of age or fitness level studies show that making time for exercise provides some serious mental benefits. Studies also show that it is very effective at reducing fatigue, improving alertness and concentration, and at enhancing overall cognitive function. Working up a sweat can help manage physical and mental stress. It is one of the best ways to clear your mind, lift mood and boost energy. Spend 20-30 minutes doing your workout. Shoot for at least 2-3 times per week. Once you begin to exercise regularly, you will discover many more reasons why exercise is so important to improving the quality of your life.

2) Create Your Own Reality

The Wright brothers wanted to fly, and people considered them lunatics.

Leonardo da Vinci, Thomas Edison and Bill Gates were considered as daydreamers, when actually, they were visualizing and imagining their vision. Whatever they were imagining years ago, is now a solid reality.. Your imagination is a gateway to the possible and a bridge to your unconscious mind. It is your preview of life's coming attraction. It's the limitless palate with which you craft your world and a built-in key to manifesting your hopes. Your subconscious mind doesn't recognize the deviation between what is genuine and what is imaginary. Your reality mirrors what goes on in your mind.

When envisioning your desire, engage your imagination by using all of your senses. Imagine not only the visualizations, but also the sounds, textures, smells and tastes of your dreams coming true. Even more significantly, think of the feelings of the outcome you look for as these contain the strongest magnetic force for drawing in your desires. How you feel about what you imagine will decide whether you'll successfully draw it in or not.

Feelings are the language that talks to the Divine Matrix (the Universe). Feel as if your goal is completed and your prayer is already responded. Rehearse the future you want to attract in your head on a regular basis. What sort of future do you desire? How would you look, act and feel? Whatever you are grasping on from your past is what you are bringing into your present reality. And whatever the mind can conceive and believe, it can accomplish. A different key element to drawing in and allowing the realities you look for is a sense of worth. If you do not feel that you deserve the truth you want, you'll block its manifestation or undermine it once it arrives. Your sense of worth reflects your level of self-value and is meddled by guilt, dishonor, self- judgment and negative self-concepts. Self-love and self-forgiveness always increase your sense of worth.

3) Adopt An Attitude Of Gratitude

Science tells us that an "attitude of gratitude" is a good health choice. Being more grateful more often makes us happier and more optimistic. Gratitude attracts what we want. The universal truth of attraction says that we will attract into life the things we think about and focus on. It can immediately transform all areas of your life.

The fastest way to attain an "abundance mind-set" and align your emotional vibration with the flow of prosperity and joy, is to adopt an attitude of gratitude. Gratitude will positively shift your energy instantly and clear out any negativity thoughts that have been accumulating throughout your day. Counting your blessings is one of the fastest ways to improve your mood or outlook.

And focus on what you do what attract even more. What you focus on expands. When you are grateful for what you have, even when it is not enough, you'll attract more of the good things in your life. Bear in mind that no matter how bad your situation or life may

5

be, there is always something to be grateful for. As soon as you find it, your life will significantly improve!

Chapter 2:

Self-Enhancement
Mantras

There's a popular saying...

"I ought to change, but I've attempted and failed." Does this seem familiar?

There's no doubt about it: change is hard. But it is essential for your growth and development as a person. Frequently, altering habits does seem insurmountable. A lot of us merely don't have enough motivation to alter our habits - all of our foul habits - in a way that would really affect our life. We hold them tight as we view them as rewards. But your habits determine your life. To break a bad habit, it's helpful to reward yourself for engaging in the positive behavior. Although the hardest part of any new habit is pulling through the first month, particularly the 1st several days. When you've made it through those first thirty days, it's much simpler to continue as you've overpowered inertia.

When we consider changing a habit for good, we frequently psych ourselves out before we start. Believing we have to give something up for a lifetime is too overpowering to even think about. Rather than making a huge change all at once, you aim to take one little step in the proper direction. When you have gotten comfy with that change, take a different little step. Go forward taking little steps one at a time till you sooner or later reach your goal. To replace the bad habits with great habits is a really good idea. Here you will find some really great habits to start that will benefit your personal development.

- Construct a fresh habit by tacking a job onto one of your habits you already have. Water the flowers after you have taken your lunch.
- Send off thank-you notes after you check your inbox
- Work out daily. Supercharge your metabolism, concentration, and mental clarity in half-hour a day.
- By choice make the job harder as challenging jobs are more engaging and motivating than ho-hum ones. Do physical chores like filing or cleaning with your non-dominant hand. Draw up poetic e-mails to answer other emails.
- Figure how long a job will take to finish. Then start a timer and press yourself to complete it in one-half that time.

- Discover individuals who are already acquiring the results you want; question them; and adopt their mental attitude, notions, and behavior.
- Finish an otherwise dull task in an uncommon or crazy manner to keep it fun and intriguing. Make routine calls utilizing fake foreign accents. Take notes in wax crayon.
- Interpose one task into the middle of some other. Study while eating lunch. Return calls while traveling back and forth to work. Listen to audio programs while shopping.
- When somebody does you a good turn, refer a thank-you card. That's a true card, not an e-card. This is uncommon and memorable, and the individuals you thank will be eager to bestow more opportunities.
- Cast out the negative people from your life; and affiliate with positive, happy individuals instead. Mentalities are catching. Be loyal to reality, affection, and might, not to pity.
- Explain your most ambitious issues to several others, and ask for all the advice, feedback, and constructive critique you are able to handle.
- On a sheet of paper, jot down twenty originative ideas for bettering your effectiveness.
- Study books and articles listen to audio programs and go to seminars to soak up fresh themes and inspiration.

Investing in yourself may be the most profitable investment you ever make. So invest more time in yourself. The effort you put into consistently investing in yourself plays a large role in determining the quality of your life now and in the future.

- When an undesirable task is assigned to you, re-delegate it to somebody else.

- Name the item on your job list that frightens you the most. Muster up all the bravery you are able to and tackle it at once.
- When an apparently senseless job is delegated to you, bounce it back to the individual who assigned it to you, and challenge them to rationalize its functional necessity.
- Quit clubs, jobs, and subscriptions that consume more of your time than they deserve. Declutter for more personal time.
- Hold up non-critical jobs as long as you potentially can. A lot of them will die and won't need to be accomplished at all.
- Switch off the television, particularly the news, and recapture a lot of available hours.
- Hire a personal coach to remain motivated, centered, and accountable.

Chapter 3:

Unlocking Your Ultimate Potential

Every speck of scientific research on the subject of human potential says that we all have much more potential power and ability than we are currently using. Do you know your true potential? Have you reached your full potential? Most of us are unaware of the accomplishments we can achieve in our lives. We become tied down to the daily routine that seems to be working, (for the most part) and settle in for the long haul. We either choose not to or do not have time to look deeper in to our true potentials. It is of paramount importance to unlock your ultimate potential...

Not realizing your true potential is probably one of the bigger regrets as people get older; realizing that you could've been more is one of the biggest emotional upheavals you can experience in your life. That is why it is quintessential that you do not let opportunities fly away; for those fortunate enough to live in a society where there is free will to do and be pretty much anything you want, you must capitalize the opportunity to self-actualize, to be the best you can be. To be the best you, here are things you can do to realize and unlock your ultimate potential:

1) Discover Your Full Potential

No matter what innate talents you were born with, what family you were born into, the money you have made or lost, or the times of difficulty or lucky breaks, nothing will get you to where you want to be better than understanding your full potential. It's the breaking factor in every successful story. The popular poor man gets lucky story, or the how I changed the world with my bare hand's tale comes from one important factor- the people who succeed are the people who learn how to tap into something innate inside them, and live and breathe their dreams.

Each one of us has potential lying innate inside of us. The brilliant part is each one of us has a potential that is uniquely ours. The potential to become a better person, to gain more respect, to be more successful, to find happiness, to achieve anything we want. It's a mad mix of our genetics, our environment, the way our body has been designed and the talents we were born with. Of course, the first step is discovering just what that is. It can be very frustrating to go on with life not knowing what you are supposed to achieve...

The world is a negative place and the forces are pulling us from every direction, learning to avoid the negativity is like learning to walk on a minefield. For some this is an instinctive process, often helped by a watchful parent or teacher that spotted something in us from an early age and called it into being. For others, it's a struggle to identify. It has been proven that we absorb most of the negativity through our unconscious mind, not even realizing it is happening. Being weighed down by your own or others negativity can destroy your chances of reaching your true potential so learn to control other people's energies as you control your destiny.

Environment can also play a part. We often learn about what we are good at through trying new things. If you lived in an area where there weren't a lot of options, or you didn't have a lot of money to pay for classes or for travel, then you may have not experienced the things you are naturally good at. The most direct way to live smarter is to evaluate your current alignment with all of the things up to now.

Take a moment and ask yourself...

- What are my gifts and talents?
- What am I good at?
- Where can I use my strengths?
- Where can I exercise my values?
- Where can I make a difference?

What makes me comfortable in life?

What is it that you can do even when you are not being paid? If we all concentrated in what we love doing, we would be happier and more fulfilled. Loving what you do gives you the strength to weather personal setbacks, face and address your weaknesses, overcome adversity and work the long hours typically needed to reach your full potential. Once you identify your values, passions and strength, it is easier for you to grow as a person and reach for your full potential. There is a connection between reaching your potential and being aware of your passions. And more often than not your passions will flow from your values and strengths. When you connect with your passions it allows you to act every day from your heart; it gives you the energy to propel you toward your goals, while overcoming setbacks and failure.

2) Unlock Your Mind Power

You may not realize it, but the mind is very powerful. It is unlimited in potential. Once you begin to understand the power of the mind, and learn the laws of the universe, you can reprogram your subconscious so you can obtain anything you want in life and live life to the fullest. Every person on this planet has the same capacity in their brain but not everyone uses it. It is really the programming that we received from birth to the present that shapes who we are and what we do.

Your mind is the projector of your current physical reality that you experience through your 5-sense reality. The subconscious mind is like your magic genie and it will accept anything that you feed to it and it will carry out your every wish. So, whatever you consistently think about whether it is real or imagined your subconscious mind will accept it is as the truth and it will work with us and for us to help us reach our goals.

Once we unlock the keys our mind holds, we have the opportunity to do the following: Learn to override the fears of failure and not being good enough. To let go of social phobias and the hold of limiting beliefs.

- Discover the talents and gifts we were given and how we can develop them.
- Learn how to spot new opportunities to develop personal growth and learn new skills.
- Set goals you had always thought were the goals of dreamers, and then meet those goals.
- Develop a strong sense of purpose and direction. Learn the value of your life in this world and what a difference your new life can make.
- Become someone who loves to face a challenge and then meet it, and overcome it. You'll discover the fun in conquering the mountains of challenge in your own life and not taking the status quo as an acceptable standard anymore.
- Learn the benefits of a balanced life where your physical, emotional, spiritual and financial health lives in harmony with each other and you feel fulfilled and satisfied with your life.
- No longer be someone who's happy to be just comfortable. You'll instead want to live in the zone of the outrageous, fulfilled and achieved. By investing in time to unlock your own potential, you have the opportunity to discover all that you were created to be.

Part of that process is identifying what your purpose is. To do that you need to first look at what makes you feel passionate. A life lived with passion is a life lived fully.

3) Find Your Passion

The most important ingredient in achieving your goals is passion. Intelligence, connections and courage may all help, but nothing can trump passion. The truly successful person is almost always one who is extremely passionate about his or her endeavor.

"Nothing great in the world has been accomplished without passion" -

Georg Hegel, German Philosopher

If you want to succeed in life, you first must find your passion, then harness it and use it to focus your dreams and vision. The more you follow the path your passion leads you down, the more you achieve the goals you desire, and your life starts to fall into place. One of the best parts of living a life of where you develop your own potential is its infectious. People want to be around someone with direction. It's like a contagious drug. You are finding your passion and purpose will affect everyone else in your life - without you even planning on it.

Think of the five or ten people you spend most time with. What are these people doing? How passionate are they? Do they inspire you? When you're passionate about your work, whether building a company or investing in real estate, others see that passion and are drawn to it. Good things come from that attraction.

Find what it is that expressly drives you and there you have your chief purpose. For instance, though you may want a lot of money - ask yourself what is it for? Is your chief goal to create a museum of your belongings? Is it to provide for your family? Or is it to have the freedom to spend your life serving a cause you believe in? All of these indicate a vastly different purpose, even if all require a large sum of money. If your purpose seems completely unrelated to making money don't worry at all! Finding purpose isn't just about finding wealth. Not everyone is wired to make money as part of their purpose. Whatever your purpose, it may not be the same as anyone else in your family or among your friends. This is about what you want to do, what you want to achieve. Allow yourself to dream your own dreams and reach your own goals.

Are the dreams you have any better or worse than another's? No. All each of us should do is live our live by the purpose we hold deep inside us. Imagine how different the world would be if that was what everyone did. What an exciting and fulfilling way to live.

4) Find Your Ultimate Purpose

As we are all different, we will all need different paths to help us find our passion and purpose. If you've struggled to find the direction you need to complete your destiny, if you've always felt you were made for something, but a little unsure what t was that try some of the following ideas to explore what your purpose may be. Everyone has a purpose, and there is potential in each of us. It's just a matter to exploring and investigating a little to discover it.

What terrifies you?

It's an interesting concept but what you don't like, or what you fear may be the very thing pointing to your destiny. It's like the concept of yin and yang- there are two sides to each coin.

The fear may originate from blocking off an early passion that you were unaware of. Write a list of your fears and the negative feelings that come from them. Then look at that list and see if there is an opposite charge to the fear. For example, if you are terrified of public speaking, but love to share your ideas, then you may be well suited to expressing yourself through the written word. When are you scared of failing? Those things that are important to us hold a great deal of weight to how we see ourselves and our success. If you are scared at failing at something, you'll often avoid it at all costs. But those things we are scared to fail at are often the very things we most want to do. Explore the times you've said no to something or avoided something because you've been scared of showing yourself to not be good at it.

Who energizes you? Stay away from people who tear or wear your down... Align yourself with people living a full life and their enthusiasm rubs off and affects your own passion. Go for people you respect, and work underneath them- serving them. That is the very best way to learn. If you can't find anyone like that around you, devour books about people you admire and learn by proxy.

(i) When Will You Get There?

Each journey starts with one small step in front of the other. The end destination isn't the only thing you need- you need to break it right down into manageable chunks.

You may start with a small passion in something really simple that you don't think much of, and then it explodes and evolves into something else entirely. Enjoy that process and trust it. Write out a list of more baby steps you can take later today, tomorrow, the next day and each day for the rest of your life. Notice how you feel as you take each step. Notice how your life is changing for the better. Find other people who want to join you on your journey. Yes, they're out there.

Just like babies taking their first steps, sometimes we need some help and sometimes we fall down. Just like a baby does, get up and keep trying until you've mastered that step. We've all been there before and know how hard it can be. The most important step is to decide to take that first step. If you are naturally visionary, having to wait it out sometimes can be incredibly frustrating. Don't get upset if you deviate from your intended destination. Sometimes diversions lead to more exciting places and experiences. Sometimes plans change. Be flexible. Be open to new experiences... By learning to temper your impatience and lay it aside helps you get there faster. Have faith in yourself that everything you work on will eventually pay off. Faith and belief are the keys to trigger the universe signal so that it knows what you truly desire...

(ii) Who Are You Now?

Before you start to move forward you need to first make peace with the person you are today, right here and right now. The person you are today is the person you started to become five or ten years ago.

We are all a product of our own past and the place we are in today is of our own making. To move forward we need to accept the person we are, with all our foibles and limitations. Love yourself now; accept yourself now and where you have been, and then move on. Our purpose can begin from any circumstances. No matter what has gone before, we have the choice to change our life now, today. One person in themselves can be hugely effective. Dream big and don't underestimate your ability to get there - many people have dreams up a purpose that on paper looked impossible but was not only achieved but surpassed. Breathe life into those big visions.

(iii) What Will You Do?

Make a list of all the dreams and thoughts you've had – all the things you want to do in your life. Once it's down on paper, make a plan of action to follow. Sometimes the first step is to consolidate, to regroup and spend some time learning or preparing. This is an excellent time to give your time to work under people who are working towards a similar purpose, to learn alongside them.

Don't worry if the times get a little rough sometimes. See the difficult times are periods of growth, where you are learning the next important lessons to succeed. There is a well-known Chinese proverb that says, "When things are going good the business grows, when things are going bad, you grow." No experience is ever wasted as long as you grasp any circumstance as an opportunity to grow.

5) Commit To Your Ultimate Purpose

Once you have established what your purpose is, write it down. Keep it as simple and as clear as possible. A three pager probably indicates you are still trying to find your purpose.

Then break your purpose down. Say for instance you felt your purpose was to become a talk show host. Consider the steps you need to achieve that. What qualifications would you need? Would you need to alter your appearance at all?

How would you go about lifting your profile so people know who you are and believe you can do what you do? Write these mini goals down on a piece of paper. Read these goals aloud every morning and night, to help you stay on track. This is your personal journey and you don't need to share it with anyone else.

The ability to harness your mind and control your thought processes is one that successful people through the ages have used. It's the common denominator of all successful people whether they are business owners or world class athletes. Research in the ability to drive past our own concept of limiting belief has shown that if we get the mind on track, the rest will follow.

Turn your life into the life you want by discovering the purpose you were born to live and then change the way you think of yourself living that life to get there. Remember the place you are now is the place you got to by the thoughts you've already had- even if it was not a conscious decision.

Start to take your future place in this world into both your conscious and subconscious mind, learning to turn around and more ahead to reach your purpose. It won't take long to enjoy the fruits of your endeavors.

Chapter 4:

Empty Your Mind

When you think, hear, speak, cry out, engage in something physical or stressful the waves are produced. With meditation everything stops. Your brain may be totally still, unmoving. It's really possible. When the surface of the brain quiets and becomes still we begin to see and feel what is underneath. We wouldn't know there's anything much underneath our consciousness except what we may see from the surface.

The basic truth about meditation is simple that you could learn it in just five minutes, and you can readily engage in it anytime and anywhere. Yet you should constantly engage in it to improve on it. Likewise, it could also be developed into a habit wherein it becomes natural or second nature to a person to engage in it. The more one practices meditation the higher the level of meditation one can achieve.

Empty Mind Meditation is a meditation technique in which the mind is gradually emptied of all thoughts which interfere in the process of meditation. Buddhists call this method Vipassana or Antiparasitic. In the ancient times, spiritual greats had used the Empty Mind method to attain enlightenment. The reason why "Empty Mind Meditation" is They devote themselves to years, sometimes an entire lifetime, of dedicated practice to achieve the state where thoughts disappear completely or no longer arise.

commonly used lies in the fact that the ultimate purpose of meditation is to attune oneself to the universal will by emptying oneself of the "ego" or the self. The mind is a powerful tool which sometimes hinders us from achieving the inner peace which we all seek. Empty Mind Meditation helps them find some relaxation from the highly demanding and hectic lifestyle in which most modern people find themselves.

The mere practice of emptying the mind enables a person to free the mind from the anxious thoughts which clutter the mind throughout the day. By achieving a relaxed state, one can de-stress the body and consequently achieve healing of some ailing body parts. The constant practice of Empty Mind Meditation is beneficial to the holistic development of oneself.

The five areas of life improved by the regular practice of Empty mind meditation are: The Physiological Aspect, the Social Aspect which involves the way we relate with other people, the Intellectual Aspect, Emotional and, the Spiritual aspect.

The Stages Of Empty Mind Meditation

An empty mind is a mind that is free from selfish thoughts. It is the primary goal of meditation to attune oneself to the universal mind by freeing the mind from any selfish thoughts. This is a simple process that most people find difficult to achieve. This is because as human beings, we tend to cling to what we have learned, striven for, and have achieved. This is exactly the opposite of letting go of all thoughts. In meditation, we will learn how to let go of these clingy thoughts. There are numerous procedures or ways to achieve and complete a meditation.

The most experienced meditation practitioner uses the simplest step-by-step procedure which is shown here:

Be seated comfortably

The first thing that a practitioner should do is to find a suitable place to meditate. Sitting is basically the most widely used position in meditation. Even Buddha himself, in most figurines and pictures, is commonly depicted seated in a cross-legged manner. You can sit on a chair, at floor, or in your bed. You can sit anywhere but what is important that you are seated comfortably with your back straightened so that your back muscles will not readily strain.

Likewise, you can use a pillow for back support and for comfort. There are several traditional sitting positions that are widely used by meditation practitioners such as the Burmese position, the Quarter Lotus, the Half Lotus, and the Full Lotus positions. These positions are popular because they can be used for long-duration meditation. When conducting lengthy meditation, it is extremely important to be in a quiet place to avoid any kind of distraction.

Relaxing the Body

The next step in the meditation process is the closing of one's eyes and the relaxing of the body by tensing, stretching, or curling one part of body repeatedly until you feel relaxed. While you are seated, push your hips forward, and then push your stomach out while tensing up all your stomach muscles for a couple of times and relaxing between to relieve the tension. Tuck your stomach in until the muscles of your lower back and buttocks are tensed enough, and then arch both your shoulders and push your chest in, tensing all your upper back muscles repeatedly. Then, slacken your muscles in between exercises. And then, reversing the exercise by pulling your shoulders back and pushing your chest out, tensing all your muscles and then slackening the tension.

This exercise relieves the upper body of stress and tension. Repeat this process until you are feeling relaxed. Then, you can start arching your neck forward and placing your chin on your chest, tensing neck and jaw muscles, then momentarily relaxing to reverse the action by pushing your head all the way back while raising your chin up high, and tensing your throat and jaw muscles. Move your head back while looking up; then, open your mouth wide and screw your face up face, tensing your facial and other muscles in your head, and tensing and relaxing. Likewise smile widely as possible, while screwing up your face and tensing all facial muscles. Frown deeply while screwing up your face; then tense all your facial muscles. This exercise relieves our muscles and joints of the stress and tensions that accumulate every day.

Breathing

The third step in the meditation process is to be aware of your breathing. Breathe deeply but silently. Use your abdomen while breathing. Feel your abdomen expands and contracts while you inhale and exhale. Inhale through your nostrils and exhale through the mouth. Moderate your breathing and give it a regular pacing until you reach a point of almost non-breathing. This will further relax the body and mind and set your being in a meditative mood.

Clearing Your Mind

As you find yourself with the correct, relaxed breathing, observe the thoughts passing through your mind. Don't interfere with these thoughts; just observe them and you will notice some gaps between two thoughts. Gently focus on the gap where there is no thought. Try to expand this thoughtless gap. Let it last longer until there is no thought anymore. This is the traditional method used by Gautama Buddha in achieving enlightenment. Another empty mind meditation procedure is by emptying the mind of any thought by thinking nothing and doing nothing. Normally thoughts suddenly come out of nowhere; just ignore them. Revert back to thinking of nothing. Just close your eyes and observe the blackness or whiteness regardless of any thoughts which may crop.

Chapter 5:

Attracting Your True Calling

There are many different people in this world. The amazing thing is the fact that each one of us has our own specific purpose in life that we are supposed to fulfill. It is very important that we find this purpose and live it. This is the key to true happiness. If true happiness is what you are seeking in life, it is not more money that you need or to become more popular. You need to discover what your true calling in life is. Therefore, to get the best out of life itself, the individual would be required to spend some time and effort to actually explore the possibility of understanding his or her true calling and working on fulfilling this call. Once you discover your purpose, you will see your life in a whole new light.

"There is no greater gift you can give or receive than to honor your calling. It's why you were born. And how you become most truly alive." Oprah Winfrey

1) Identify True Calling

Have you discovered your calling? The reason you are alive. Your personal mission in life. If you do not have a clue what I am discussing, take a couple seconds to complete this quick quiz:

- What do I really, really want in life?
- Am I doing precisely the kind of work that makes me want to jump out of bed every morning?
- Am I doing what I love?
- If I achieve all my goals, what would it look like?

If you have a clear answer to all of these questions, congratulations! There is a good chance that you've achieved what the Buddhist's call "Right Livelihood." If you have not yet found the work you were meant to do, keep reading. You are about to find your true calling – and when you find that calling that is uniquely yours, your life will be transformed.

2) 7 Tips to Finding Your Calling

Most people go through life doing a job just to get the pay check at the end of the month. Most spend nearly all of it on bills and rarely do something they actually like. Others are happy at work and have large amount of money. However, for the vast majority this is but a dream yet to be fulfilled. Have you realized that the most successful people are invariably those people who spend the most time thinking about who they are and where they are going, and then constantly evaluating and re-evaluating their progress in light of who they are and what they really want?

Hence, the starting point of great success is for you to realize that you are truly extraordinary! You were put on this earth to do something wonderful with your life. There has never been anyone in the entire universe just like you. You have remarkable skills, aptitudes, abilities, insights and ideas that make you different, and in some way, superior to all other people who have ever lived. And it is your job is to find out what that wonderful thing is and then to throw your whole heart into doing it extremely well. Your life may have a single purpose, like that of Mother Theresa of Calcutta, or your life may have multiple, sequential purposes, one after the other as you evolve and grow and develop into a higher and better person. The path to our calling is an evolving process.

To get the best out of life itself, the individual would be required to spend some time and effort to actually explore the possibility of understanding his or her true calling and working on fulfilling this call. Being able to deal positively and honestly with the feelings and thoughts will help the individual better identify the inner voice that is so in tune with the true calling meant for him or her. Taking the time to stop and think really hard about what really excites, stimulates and interests you will help to narrow down the quest to finding the true calling you were designed to embark upon.

(i) What Am I Good At?

Things you can do so easily that you hardly notice them. It could be things like...

- Understanding how to bring a group of people back into harmony
- Great at organizing events and connecting with others
- Picking the right stocks to invest in
- Being able to quote movie dialog word for word
- Sensing how to comfort someone

Everyone is born with innate gifts and talents. Every one of us has different skills that help us to become successful at one thing or another. What's something you're good, dare I say, amazing at?

- Create great marketing proposals
- Great at money management

When you are looking for your true calling in life, you must sit down and determine what these skills are. You need to know what you are good at, as it will help you to look in the right direction. Pay attention to the compliments people around you give as it is a clear message of your skills and will help you know which path you should consider pursuing.

(ii) Do Some Reflection On Past Callings

- What elements of your past success came from times when you cared the most about what you were doing?

Analyzing your past success can bring you great rewards in the future, as it helps you learn from your mistakes and success so you can find your true career path in life.

(iii) Stay in The Present

While trying to discover what your calling in life is, it is extremely important that you make sure that you keep your mind in the present. Do not focus on the future. Everything we do today will affect our future and that is why it is so important that we are always focused on the here and now. Life is lived one second at a time so there is no reason to stress about five years from now.

(iv) Try Different Things

You have to get out of your comfort zone or your "safety bubble". Staying in your comfort zone will not give the opportunity to try new things. The problem with this is the fact that you will never be able to discover what your true calling is if you do not ever get the opportunity to try it. Do not be afraid to try something new. Finding your true calling often involves trial and error. Take a chance and launch out into something you suspect might be your true calling. You may just succeed and discover greater satisfaction and purpose for your life. Even if you fail, you can learn more about yourself and which avenues you should pursue in the future.

(v) Track Challenges

Track the challenges in your life and unravel the common threads. You will definitely feel like what you are doing with your life is purposeful when you are constantly challenging yourself. Your challenges are your instructors. They show you the places you need to heal and grow so that you are able to become who you are meant to be.

- **Are you struggling with:** Finding your sense of self-worth? Trusting the Universe and trusting others? Feeling bombarded by life and like nothing works out for you?

- **These clues tell you:** What you need to work on - How you going to inspire others - What you have chosen to master in this life time

(vi) Talk to Those Who Listen

Share your dreams and desires with those that you trust and listen to what you are saying. Also try and speak with people who offer real feedback and ideas and stay away from those who simply agree with what you are saying or give you one-word responses. Other people can have some very valuable insight, especially the elderly so it may be a good idea to ask them for advice on discovering your calling in life. They may notice talents that you have that you are not aware of.

(vii) Live Your Own Dream

Learn how to live and create your own dreams. Do not look at others and envy them for what they have or wish that you could have their life and their blessings. You need to figure out what your true desires are in life and what you truly want. No one else is going to pursue your dreams for you. Everyone has their own dreams and their own goals for what they want to achieve in life. If you don't go for it, no one else will. By this I do not mean material objects, I mean what you want from life and what you want your life to be. Stop trying to live someone else's dream... Discover your true purpose and find the courage to live your own dream!

3) 7 Tips to Help You Follow Through

When we have goals, we have our destinations in each period of our life. Whether we will get to those destinations depends on our actions. In order to have the right actions, we need to have a plan. It is however difficult for many individuals to follow through their plan despite the need to accomplish their goals. What are the reasons why they cannot follow through?

When we have goals, we have our destinations in each period of our life. Whether we will get to those destinations depends on our actions. In order to have the right actions, we need to have a plan. It is however difficult for many individuals to follow through their plan despite the need to accomplish their goals. What are the reasons why they cannot follow through?

One of the most common reasons that make individuals do not follow through is that they are not willing to be out of their comfort zone. Humans are creatures of comfort. Being in one's comfort zone implies familiarity, safety, and security. It describes the patterned world of our existence, keeps us relatively comfortable and calm, and helps us stay emotionally even, free from anxiety and worry to a great degree.

We need to realize how important it is to step out of comfort zone. The disadvantage of remaining in your comfort zone is that you will never grow within it. You have to start living outside your comfort zone to grow physically, mentally, spiritually, financially and on the relationships with other people. We must practice our mind to get used to working our way towards our goals despite feeling uncomfortable. The following seven tips will assist you in following through with your plan.

(i) Acknowledge What You Want and Why You Want It

You need to know what you want out of your actions and the reasons why you want it. I see many people around me who don't get what they want, precisely because they don't even acknowledge their desires to begin with. These are the self-deniers. You will not be prompted to do what you are supposed to do if you are not clear on what you want. Clarity is your power to go to your target. Be clear on your goals. Without goals you lack focus and direction. Goal setting not only allows you to take control of your life's direction; it also provides you a benchmark for determining whether you are actually succeeding. You have to decide what you want and then make the dedication to achieving it.

(ii) Decide What You Love to Do

Your actions to your goals will have to be repeated it again and again. If you do not love what you do, it is very hard to continue doing. Your brain will tell yourself that you have no fun doing it. This is why individuals give up a lot easier than they are supposed to. Many individuals said they do not have option. On the contrary, they do not really decide to do what they love. Rather, they let themselves in doing what they do not like. It is up to your decision to stop what you think you must do and go to the area that you love most.

(iii) Take Action

Another thing that happens to many individuals is that when they want something, they do not even bother to begin doing something. Absolutely nothing is more important than being proactive. You must take action and begin by doing something. Action, the process or state of acting or being active, is what makes it all happen. So whether a person is trying to be happy, be wealthy, lose weight or even start a new business, it all starts with an action. The process of being in a state of action is irreplaceable; action is that one thing that makes it all possible. You are able to do anything by beginning to do something that is aimed at your goal. The most difficult part is always the first step. Once you have the first step, other steps will be a great deal easier for you.

(iv) Keep Your Momentum

To have great success, momentum must be created. Once you begin doing something, do not let your actions die afterwards. Keep doing what is in your plan. Do not let your mind fly away while you take action. But, set goals that are specific with progress measurements along the way. You are able to reward yourself for your hard work. Avoid beating yourself up if you fall short. Take baby steps, one at a time. You are also able to make a vision board, or some goal vision note to see as often as you want.

If you're setting about the job of producing a vision board, you might discover yourself taking steps that will open you up mentally and let you relax and feel originative in order to discover those inner wants. It helps to ignite clarity. to maintain your momentum through the year, you need to set powerful, crystal-clear goals By selecting pictures and writing that charges your emotions with feelings of passion, you will begin to manifest those things into your life.

(v) Value Your Actions and Results

Review your actions and see if you need to correct anything. Make sure you keep track of your progress and measure it constantly. Keep your statistic and compare with the standard. Change your approach if you need to but never change your goals.

(vi) Perseverance

What separates a person from achieving their goals and not achieving their goals is staying focused and being persistent in following through Most of the important things in the world have been accomplished by people who have kept on trying when there seemed to be no hope at all. - Dale Carnegie Perseverance is one of the key qualities that you need to reach success. Frequently this factor alone is the difference between failure and success. Perseverance is also a personal value, because it gives shape and strengthens your character which allows you to keep your focus on your goal.

Not giving up is one of the best qualities of successful people. You need to make sure that you also have that quality. Commit to yourself that you will not give up no matter what happens.

(vii) Visualize Your Success Regularly

Visualization will make your subconscious mind attract what you want into your life. This is according to the Attraction Mantra Secrets. You can attract all situations and attributes favorable to your goal achievement by visualization daily. Visualize in your mind as if you are achieving your goals in front of you. Feel it and absorb what happens. You may want to add the background audio while you are visualizing. It will enhance your attraction.

4) Putting it all together

Is there something you already love doing? Do you have a hobby, or something you loved doing as a child, but never considered it as a possibility? Whether it's reading comic books, collecting something, making something, creating or building, there is probably a way you could do it for a living. Open a comic book shop or create a comic book site online. If there's already something you love doing, you're ahead of the game. Now you just need to research the possibilities of making money from it. Brainstorm. Nothing comes to mind right away. Well, get out a sheet of paper, and start writing down ideas. Anything that comes to mind, write it down. Look around your house, on your computer, on your bookshelf, for inspirations, and just write them down. There are no bad ideas at this stage. Write everything down and evaluate them later. Ask around, and surf for possibilities. Ask other people for ideas. See what others have discovered as their passions. Look all over the Internet for ideas. The more possibilities you find, the more likely your chances of finding your true passion.

Do as much research as possible. Know as much about your passion as possible. If this has been a passion for a while, you may have already been doing this. At any rate, do even more research. Read every website possible on the topic and buy the best books available. Either find other people, in your area or on the Internet, what do you want to do for a living, and quiz them about the profession. How much do they make? What training and education did they need? What skills

are necessary? How did they get their start? What recommendations do they have? Often you will find that people are more than willing to give advice. Never quit trying. Can't find your passion at first? Give up after a few days and you're sure to fail. Keep trying, for months on end if necessary and you'll find it eventually.

Found your passion but haven't been successful making a living at it? Do not give up. Keep trying, and try again, until you succeed.

Success does not come easy, so giving up early is a sure way to fail. Keep trying, and you will get there. You also want to keep your health in very good standing. It definitely always helps to keep your stress levels down. Health is important because you feel better about the things you are doing, which lead to finding your true calling. Being stress free has to be the most important though. The reason being is you have a clear mind. Your head is not cluttered with things that are mundane and tedious. If you get rid of that stress, it is easier to focus on what you're really want, your true calling.

Chapter 6:

'Force' The Universe to Give You What You Want

The items we're attracted toward, tell a lot about us, after all we're about our attraction. Note, here I'm substituting thoughts with attraction. We in preset are the residue result of the preceding thoughts or attractions. Put differently we in the here and now are the manifestation of our preceding or recent thoughts or attractions. Isn't it intriguing, the cause and effect mechanism, "what we are in the here and now are caused by preceding thoughts", this incredible fact arms us with the might to manifest what we seriously want, by drawing in them in the present? Attraction Mantra Secrets is a beautiful phenomenon. Isn't it?

Here are the 3 steps to 'Force' the universe to give you what you want:

1) Accept Responsibility

What you go through is definitely your own. I may talk over your life with you, I may understand your situation, and I may do my best to you. But afterwards I may go home to my own life and forget about yours. You don't have that luxury. If you want to be successful, you have to take 100% responsibility for everything that you experience in your life. This includes the level of your achievements, the results you produce, the quality of your relationships, the state of your health and physical fitness, your income, your debts, your feelings—everything! This is not easy. It's not always pleasant to take responsibility for our life and circumstances, especially when those circumstances are unfavorable or completely out of our direct control. However, when you fail to take responsibility you put yourself at a clear disadvantage.

You are disadvantaged because you are resigned to the fate that you are powerless and incapable of making things better. Remember that you are responsible for yourself, whether you like it or not. No one is racing to save you. No one will hand you the ultimate job, and no one will work out your relationship issues. No one will lose the additional blubber on your body. If you don't proactively work out your own issues, they'll never be worked out.

If you wish changed results, you have to go out and produce them yourself. Taking on total responsibility for your life signifies being willing to accomplish what's necessary to produce the result you want. You have to be willing to ante up the price to meet your needs and satisfy your wants. You have to actively make your life story occur rather than passively allowing it to play out. You'll certainly make errors along the way, but you have to never quit on yourself.

The silver lining is that while embracing complete responsibility may be really ambitious, it isn't unattainable. You might not have had much command over your outcomes up to now, but the dedication to develop you might give you the chance to at last produce a life of your choosing. Your mortal will be far more potent than any obstacle in your path. You'll certainly meet challenges and setbacks while going after worthwhile goals, but if you merely continue your willingness to ante up the price, you'll sooner or later succeed.

2) Being Dedicated

If you hear someone state that success is easy, hightail it as fast as you are able to as you're about to hear a sales pitch for some product. The honest truth is that it's truly hard to win at something you've never executed previously. But that's absolutely all right. Get the picture that that failure and success aren't opposites. If you bomb, it signifies you're taking action, so you're making mistakes and training yourself. Success occurs by nature once you finally learn how to take the right actions. What do you desire? What are your fantasies? What do you long for so severely that you can't quit thinking of it, even if you believe it unimaginable? Let yourself dream. Cultivate your richest desires, regardless how impractical or unimaginable they appear. It's absolutely all right to wish the unimaginable. It's not all right to make-believe that your wants don't matter.

Take one step at a time. Be patient with yourself as you experience failure. When you're pursuing a goal you truly want, the sort that nearly brings you to tears when you consider it as you connect with it so deeply, then you have to persist with it. Regardless how hard it gets, don't stop. Don't press yourself to achieve massive success at the beginning. Merely do the best you are able to. At the start, your best may be scarcely one notch above total half-wit -if you're lucky. Sooner or later you'll earn a little basic competence. And farther down the road, people will call you an authority-an authority being an person whose failed enough to win at getting what they want. It's incredible inspiring to watch individuals battle through one failure after some other without resigning. From the exterior looking in, it may appear as if they can't possibly succeed. However they still hang in.

Finally they learn what they have to learn. They successfully align their anticipations to fit reality, and finally their actions start bringing on the intended results. I'm struck by those who I can see are bound for greatness, but no one else realizes it yet. The revealing sign is always the same- persistence. If you're clear about what you want, settle for nothing less. Admit that success will take time, maybe much longer than you'd like. Free yourself of the fast and simple, something-for-nothing mentality.

3) Law of Visualization

Did you know that thoughts are made of pure energy? Ever had a song in your head and the next thing you know, someone around you starts humming that tune and you go, "Hey I was just thinking about that song!" Our thoughts have the ability to affect others. Our thoughts are like transmission signals. When you think about something, you transmit it out into the universe - it is as simple as that. The more you focus your thoughts on something, you start to manifest it. Think of it like the power of concentration. To make something real, you have to spend more time concentrating on it. The longer you focus on a single thing, it is likely to come true whether you are aware of it or not. Here are a few examples of how it works in reality.

If you focus on poverty, you will attract poverty... If you focus on love, you will receive love. So, at the end of the day you attract whatever you focus upon. You see in this world; we believe there is such a thing as positive thoughts and negative thoughts. However, the universe doesn't discriminate if a thought is positive or negative.

Like the magnet the mind not only attracts, but also repels. If you do not believe you can get or accomplish something, then you repel it. Thoughts of incompetence, weakness, fear and inferiority create a repellent force. It is as if you are creating a wind that blows away and prevents certain things to reach you.

Everything is just a thought to the universe. So, if you focus on positive thought, you will attract a lot of positive things from the universe. So, if you focus on a negative thought, you will attract a lot of negative things from the universe. Therefore, you have to visualize your desire to attract your desire. Know what you want and start manifesting it... Our emotion plays a big part of any visualization exercise and it is important to start with good positive thoughts and feelings. When we feel good, we can attract more feelings of feeling good. tool that is used to create reality through daydreaming, mental Visualization is an easy rehearsals, imagination and fantasizing. However, with the lack of power of these images, visualization is usually used to created unwanted experiences where the greatest fears are mentally rehearsed over and over in the minds

(i) Create A Vision Board

Write down your goals and then find images that match those goals. Create a vision board using magazines and cut out the words and images that resonate with you. The purpose of your vision board is to bring everything on it to life. Create a sacred space that displays what you want actually does bring it to life.

(ii) Feel the emotion

If the thoughts are the formulation of your desire, the emotions give them context. The key is to create an alignment of your thoughts and emotions. Act as if you already possess the things pictured on your vision board - the house, the car, or your business. Say, "this" is already mine. Imagine that you want to manifest one billion dollars. What emotion does that thought evoke in you? Can you feel complete joy and gratitude for having that kind of money? State your goals in the present tense like you have already achieved them.

(iii) Repetition

Look at the images on your vision board over and over. If you visualize consistently, you will become more motivated to do the things that will get you at least closer to what you're dreaming about, you'll be getting inspired as to what to do - you will be getting hunches to act upon. Repetitiveness of vision combined with your associated emotions will develop your power to visualize and take action to achieve your goals.

Chapter 7:

Wealth Attraction Mantra

For the record, a lot of problems arise in our lives are probably due to poverty. Did you know that we have 1000s of thoughts running through our brains on a daily basis? The crucial thing is to hone and center those thoughts and feelings on what we wish, so that what we wish will come along!

The reason most individuals are not rich is because they have damaging associations and notions about money. If you think that money is root of all evil, money makes you vicious, or that money is difficult to acquire, or that anybody who is rich must have conned somebody, or that individuals who have money selfish, then naturally, you're not going to draw in prosperity to your life. If you're constantly complaining about being poor, you will only attract more poverty. In fact, if you obsess about anything you don't have, you'll most likely continue not to have it.

Illustration, "I wish to be powerful whole and complete within myself" and "I don't wish to wind up sad and lonely" may seem like 2 ways of saying the same thing. They're not. To your subconscious mind, they're saying the opposite. Your subconscious mind doesn't understand the difference between "I wish" and "I don't wish." It simply hears "powerful whole and complete" or "sad and lonely." Therefore, if you would like to use your Attraction Mantra Secrets to produce the wealth and prosperity you want, you have to do it correctly. When you start centering on wealth as simply energy that you may easily flow into your life, you'll be astonished at how easily it turns up.

1) The Right Mindset About Money

That is the reason it becomes vital to know what kind of mindset you must have. If we try to implement the Attraction Mantra Secrets to this concept, we must realize that a person who is actually trying to attract money should think about it all the time. Since thoughts attract results, this is what must happen.

However, the thoughts mustn't be objective. What are objective thoughts? Now, if you are only thinking about how many dollars you will earn on a particular project, then that is objective thinking. If you cannot think beyond numbers, all you are doing is thinking objectively. You are thinking how much you could make, how much you could save, etc. These are objective thoughts and, if you were to apply the Attraction Mantra Secrets, you would understand that these thoughts won't attract the money to you.

Hence, you need to think subjectively. Don't think about the money itself but think about what you must do in order to bring the money to you. Thinking about the quality of your product, for example, is a beautiful step in this regard. When you do that, you are actually improving the sales potential of your product and hence you are bringing in the money. A person who believes in the Attraction Mantra Secrets won't think – "I must sell out my coaching program because I want to earn money." Instead, such a person would think – "I must provide values to my coaching students so that I can earn money out of it."

A person believing in the Attraction Mantra Secrets automatically becomes honest because he or she knows what it takes to bring in the money. They don't believe in quick-fix solutions but always go for the long haul. This should be your mindset about money too – Don't think about how to actually bring in the money; think about what you must do in order to let the money come to you.

2) Wealth Manifestation Through the Wealth Attraction Mantra

Here are the four things you need to do in order to attract the wealth that you are expecting through the Wealth Attraction Mantra. All you have to do is to apply these four simple steps to manifest money and wealth:

(i) Believe

The first step is to truly believe that you can obtain the wealth you want in life. You have to ingrain the thought of wealth in your subconscious. You have to think staunchly that you will be able to attain the large amount of wealth that you are longing for. The more you believe in your desire as a done deal and

(ii) Visualize

You have to visualize your desire to attract your desire... Use your mind to project your future, a mental image of you realizing your goal.

Don't get me wrong... It isn't about seeing yourself up on a movie screen. You aren't watching a picture from outside. You are in that movie playing the role you want to, seeing through your eyes, hearing through your ears and tasting work up your emotions about this being true, the more manifesting becomes easier. through your mouth. You visualize yourself getting the results you desire. It's as if your visualization is your only reality.

For instance, it is very important for you to actually visualize the amount of wealth you desire. You have to think that the wealth is already in your bank account and feel the emotions you are expected to feel when you receive the wealth. Begin thinking as if you are planning what to do with the money.

(iii) Be Grateful

Taking your belief one step forward, you must actually start thanking the universe for granting the wealth to you. Build an attitude of gratitude and think of how happy and grateful you will be to have the wealth you desire.

(iv) Continue Your Actions

Never give up, be relentless. Remember that stopping is a sign of weakness. You don't want the universe to understand that your belief is faltering. You want it to know that you will keep up no matter what. Sooner or later, your supreme confidence is going to bring the wealth at your door.

Instead of contemplating gratitude for the future, you need to envision it in the present. When the emotions and thoughts that correspond with genuine gratitude increase your energy, you are sharing in the universal laws that can bring you whatever you want.

3) Balance Yourself Between Inner Stillness and Outer Creation

One of the most significant applications of the Wealth Attraction Mantra is to balance our inner and outer selves. Our inner self is our consciousness. It is the way we think and behave. It is connected with the energy of the creator which is our outer self.

The way we act and implement our thought processes is how our outer self-functions.

If we have to make the best utilization of the Wealth Attraction Mantra into our life, then it is essential that we learn how to create the balance between our inner and outer selves. It is vital that we put into action what we think. That is the core driver. What begins as a thought manifestation must get converted into action.

The Wealth Attraction Mantra will make things happen. But it will restrict itself to aligning things in a particular way. Therefore, if you are feeling the urge to take actions with the hopes of getting some sort of outcome, make sure your actions are aligned with what you want.

Chapter 8:

Health Attraction Mantra

Even if you have a million dollars in the bank, it all amount to nothing if you don't have the health and vitality to use them. Did you know that the thing most affected by optimism is physical health? Logically, the body is controlled by the brain. If the brain thinks positively, that energy will radiate into the body as well.

The key to unlock the Health Attraction Mantra is to maintain high positive vibrations and a passionate, emotional state about your desires and intentions. This all begins with your beliefs and your thoughts.

Hence, you should never underestimate the power of positive thinking on your health. Positive thinking can transform your mental life, boosting your daily happiness levels and expediting your path to success. The benefits of a more positive outlook can also extend to your physical health in some interesting and surprising ways.

Researchers continue to explore the effects of positive thinking and optimism on health. Optimism doesn't mean that you have a constant grin, but it does mean remaining positive about what's to come. As Suzanne Segerstrom, a professor of psychology at the University of Kentucky, puts it: "Happiness is an emotion, a feeling. Optimism is a belief about the future."

Here are some positive effects that Health Attraction Mantra could have on your health:

1) Increased Life Span

Living longer is something we can all be happier about. A positive outlook can influence more than just your mood. People who are optimistic are more committed to their goals, are more successful in achieving their goals, are more satisfied with their lives, and have better mental and physical health when compared to more pessimistic people. Positive thinkers are keener to eat healthy foods, engage in regular exercise and practice forms of preventative healthcare.

Did You Know That...

1) One remarkable study of over 600 hospital patients in Denmark found that the people with the most positive moods were close to 60% more likely to live for at least five more years...

2) Researchers at the University of Pittsburgh School of Medicine analyzed data from nearly 100,000 women in an ongoing study funded by the National Institutes of Health. The optimistic women were 30 percent less likely to die from heart disease than the pessimists. The negative-thinking women were 23 percent more likely to die from cancer.

3) A recent medical journal article that documented the link between optimism and higher levels of good cholesterol may be explained by this interest in healthy living. A similar hypothesis showed that positive thinkers suffer from fewer heart attacks and are approximately 9% less likely to have a stroke.

By focusing on the good in life and making it your mission to take a constructive approach to problems, you set yourself up for a happier, longer life.

2) Positive Thinking Could Improve Your Immunity

Your mind can have a powerful effect on your body. Immunity is one area where your thoughts and attitudes can have a particularly powerful influence.

Optimism doesn't just boost your mood.

Did you know that a glass-half-full attitude also strengthens the immune system? Fascinating research on the connections between physical and mental health support the (initially perplexing) claim that positive thinking can boost resistance to disease.

Did you know that in one study, researcher found that people with upbeat attitudes catch fewer cold and flu viruses and show that patients who are diagnosed with potentially terminal illnesses tend to experience more consistent and significant improvements after receiving treatments?

Positive thinkers who are happier or more optimistic about their dreams and goals have a stronger immune response. They tend to react in healthier ways to stress, helping them to recover more quickly.

3) Positive Thinkers Cope Better with Stress

Positive people tend to handle things better than negative people. They are able to concentrate better in finding solutions instead of being distracted by negative elements. Moreover, the way people think also have a direct impact on their health. That is why if you conquer negative thoughts, you will have a lower chance of suffering from different kinds of diseases. Aside from this, you can also face any stressful situation with an improved focus. This helps you worry less and cope better.

Did you know that...

1) People with high stress levels are known to increase blood pressure and are related to an increased risk of health problems like diabetes and dementia?

2) A cardiovascular test on optimists and pessimists show that optimistic people's bodies return to a relaxed state (including a normal resting heart rate) at a much faster pace?

3) Men and women who reported having a happy mood (positive thoughts) had lower levels of the stress hormone cortisol?

This suggests that optimism may reduce biological vulnerability and this ability to handle stress could lead to significant health benefits... How to Unlock The Health Attraction Mantra? Now that you already know the positive effects Health Attraction Mantra can have on your health. I'm pretty sure you're excited to know the ways to unlock the Health Attraction mantra. It's pretty simple. All you have to do is to follow these 3 simple steps to unlock your Health Attraction Mantra:

1) Set Goals

Set goals to give you a sense of direction and to improve your outlook on life. You need to have clear goals in order to unlock the health attraction mantra. Write down a detailed description of exactly what you want to accomplish. By doing so, it requires you to get a well-defined mental image first. The very process of putting your thoughts into words creates clarity.

For instance, cutting down 20 pounds in three months. Perhaps you have been trying to lose 20 pounds for years but have never succeeded. In the past, you've decided to do it multiple times, but you simply never followed through. using the health attraction mantra, can now achieve this goal with much less effort, suffering, and internal struggle. You can start by fixing your focus on the goal: weight loss. Decide that it is something you need to do. Find reasons to support this goal; and constantly remind yourself of these reasons.

It could be :

- To be healthier

- To not be remembered as the fat one

- To boost up your confidence level

- To surpass the limits you thought you had

Once you have truly accepted that this goal is worthy of the struggle it will bring, move into the second phase, the visualization phase.

2) To Visualize Those Goals Being Actualized

Imagine how you will lose that weight. Visualize yourself working hard in the gym and following a strict diet plan that require sacrifice. These are all important things to see and to realize. And there's no better way to do it than using the Health Attraction Mantra. Just remember: if you want to attract a slimmer version of yourself into your life, then you will need to fix your mind on that image. If you want yourself to have body of Victoria Secret's models. All you have to do is to imagine yourself having that body and fix your mind on that image.

3) To Accept The Actualization Of Those Goals As It Occurs

Open yourself to the realization of the goal. Visualize how making these changes will improve your life. See yourself in the future after you have slimmed down. Do you feel healthier? Do you feel happier? Do you feel more attractive and self-confident?

You might be feeling uneasy but the final stage of the activation of the Health Attraction Mantra involves becoming comfortable with the realization of your goals. And this is precisely what you have to do if you wish to attain your goal and to be successful. Up until now, you have been projecting yourself into this vision that exists in the future, but let's reverse that. Instead of projecting yourself into a future reality, allow yourself to receive that reality in the   present.

Chapter 9:

Affection Attraction Mantra

All humans are created with the natural need to give and receive affection. We're created in love which forms the basis of our divine spiritual selves, and of our physically manifested life. Even the many limits that we encounter in our early lives don't remove affection from our spiritual center, because it's the essence of who we are. The quality of affection is truly universal - as it literally transcends peoples, nations and religions.

Affection is truly the universal language of this world and individuals from all different walks of life acknowledge it for what it truly is and comprehend the power that is in it.

- Take a moment and ask yourself...
- Have you activated your affection attraction mantra?
- Are you showing enough affection or lack of affection?
- Are you surrounding yourself with love that brings favorable energy into your life?
- Well, if your answer is no, you are not alone.

In fact, I am going to share with you the 4 important tips to activating your Affection Attraction Mantra:

1) Connect

In order to develop as a human, you have to master the artistry of forming connections. It is one of the most important areas of our lives. Without human connection, our lives are simply incomplete.

Do you recall how you first found out about the physical world when you were a young kid? You looked around and observed things that seized your attention. Then you proceeded towards them, grasped up, and began playing with them. You found out about your surroundings by direct, hands-on experience. If you discovered something you did not like, you attempted to avoid it in the future. If you discovered something you admired, you provided it even more tending. Occasionally your focus placed you in a state of affection.

As grownups we frequently blank out that the best way to satisfy our desires is to waltz right up to whatever intrigues us and engage with it straight off. Rather, we make all kinds of goofy principles that confine our ability to relate with what we wish. We can't begin our own business as it's too hazardous. We can't speak to that individual as we're already engaged in a relationship. We can't research other belief systems as our present religion forbids it.

Such principles are rooted in fearfulness and disconnection, and they've no place in a life story of conscious development. When you make the dedication to live consciously, you'll frequently discover yourself are not connecting on a regular basis with others it can lead to loneliness, isolation, depression and illness. When we battling with the principles. If you want to become more loving, you have to be wishing to connect.

In order to discover and grow, you have to be freed to connect with what you wish and to unplug from what you don't wish. No one may provide you that freedom. It's your right as a human. You don't require anybody's permission to choose which associations are most beneficial for you. It's up to you to accept the initiative to associate with what you wish and to unplug from what you don't wish. By consciously arriving at connections that feel intuitively right to you, you direct yourself into the right spot with the rationale of affection.

2) Communicate

Communication is such an important element in life. Think about it, we communicate with other people, with ourselves, and with the Universe. There isn't a single area of life where communication doesn't take a major role in how things go.

You communicate effectively by firstly associating with the familiar and then broadening into the unfamiliar. When you meet somebody new, the opening move is to find out your shared concerns, values, and mental attitude. This produces a basic adherence of trust and friendship. The following measure is to research and learn from your differences. Individuals who are too dissimilar from you are hard to bond with, and those who are too similar like you can't help you grow. The most beneficial relationships supply enough mutual ground to forge a strong bond while as well arousing growth in fresh directions. The deepest form of communicating is common face-to-face conversation. This lets you find out not only content but likewise vocal aspects and body language. You'll commonly experience much richer associations with individuals when you communicate in the flesh rather than by telephone or email.

Great communicating skills take time to formulate. The more you rehearse, the better you'll become. While there are particular methods you may learn like smiling, sustaining an open posture, and attaining eye contact, don't forget that the main purpose of communicating is to produce a connection with the other individual. Even when you've a particular agenda in mind such as persuasion, training, or amusement, your opening move is to institute a bond.

Excellent public speakers, instructors, and entertainers endeavor to break the ice and associate with their audiences first of all; only after this has been accomplished do they go into their primary material. True communicating calls for mutual understanding rooted in affection and faith; otherwise, you can't in effect share truth with other people.

It isn't adequate to speak your mind and presume others comprehend and accept what you're stating, nor is it adequate to listen well and assume you comprehend what's been stated. To communicate advantageously, there must be some bond between talker and listener.

There are few better delights in life than the experience of conscious communicating with another individual. No self-importance games, false fronts, or manipulative maneuvers are utilized. Both people merely wish to connect with one another for the propose of learning and developing. When you've went through such exposed, loving communicating with another human, it's difficult to go with anything less.

3) Sharing

Sharing is the deep sensation of bonding that brings about the emotional side of affection. It's the delectable feeling of completeness that stems from portioning out our real selves. Humans have been sharing for longer than we can remember... When you comprehend that there's no such thing as an extraneous relationship and that all such associations subsist entirely in your brain, you will become well aware that the real aim of relationships is self- exploration.

If you communicate in any manner, you're in truth researching different facets of yourself. Once you feel a rich sense of sharing with another individual, you're in reality connecting profoundly with a crucial part of yourself. Think about your relationship with another individual. Where does it in reality exist? It does not exist anyplace in the outside world. You can't merely point to it and state, "This is our relationship right here." It lives strictly inside your thoughts.

The great news is that when you comprehend that all relationships are internal, you are able to consciously alter how you see them and thereby alter how they go as well. If you feel disconnected with your real self, you are able to expect your personal relationships to suffer from a disconnect too. If you wish your relationships to be more loving and accepting, you have to discover how to love and live with more facets of yourself.

Loving yourself totally and unconditionally is the outcome of a conscious selection. You are free to arrive at this choice in each moment of each day. You do not need to satisfy any conditions or fulfill any rules. However in order to make this choice consciously, you have to get to know yourself. Regardless what concealed qualities you come across, you're still worthy of affection.

4) Self Love

I'm sure you've heard it before–if you want to attract love, you have to love yourself first.

Makes sense, doesn't it?

Yet, often people have difficulty in caring for themselves, in receiving love, in believing they deserve to be happy. Imagine for a moment the amount of energy you expend brooding over the future, ruminating about the past, comparing yourself to others, judging yourself, worrying about what might happen next. That is a huge amount of energy. Now imagine all of that energy gathered in and returned to you. Underlying our usual patterns of self-preoccupation, stinging self- judgment, and fear is the universal, innate potential for love and awareness.

How do you feel?

Good?

Self love is a magnet for love. It attracts happiness. The more you love yourself, the more loving people and situations will be attracted to you. Every time you do something kind to yourself, it sends a message to the Universe that you feel worthy of kindness..and guess what? More kindness will come to you! The Affection Attraction Mantra picks up your emotions. The more joy and love you feel the more positive your emotions. Doing things that make yourself happy radiates joy out to the Universe, attracting more!

Self-love makes you want to take better care of you... When matters are tough or you're combating with something, encouragement is a marvelous means of presenting you a boost... But... Do you really think encouragements have to come from somebody externally?

No, definitely not.

We can't expect people to be there for us all the time. So why not practice self-talk or self-chatter? I think we ought to always have enough favorable belief in ourselves to carry us through. Belief is empowering... Be kind to yourself, love yourself more. As you give yourself more love, you'll enjoy the nurturing things you do for yourself. That makes you self-nurture, the more loving feelings develop and the better the message you send for the Affection Attraction Mantra to respond to.

Chapter 10:

Overflowing Abundance

In this chapter we'll talk about the ways to activating overflowing abundance to shower abundance not only onto yourself, but also onto everyone around you. Talking about abundance, have you ever asked yourself "what is abundance" and how can it manifests in your life? If you haven't asked or haven't had the key to "force" the universe to give you anything you ask fo**r...** Then you are at the right place. Now before we talk about abundance, there is something you should know. It's the power of gratitude. You hear the word "gratitude" so often but take a moment and ask yourself... When was the last time you actually count your blessings or acknowledging things that you receive and notice those simple pleasures in life?

Majority of us are so busy with our lives that most of the time, we are not aware on continuous bases about how much we have been given. Now, why is it important to be grateful? Because gratitude shifts your focus from the things you lack in life towards great abundance that is now present. It is the key that unlocks the gateway to abundance. Being thankful and appreciating life and the things life offers you make us more resilient and even happier. Let me share with you the 5 steps to unlock the gateway to abundance:

1) Discover The Power Of Gratitude To Unleash Unlimited Abundance

Faced with busy schedules and challenging lives, we often forget how fortunate we truly are. Even when things are going well, we forget. Being grateful should be treated as an important part of the day because appreciation contributes to our genuine happiness. Once you develop an attitude of a sincere attitude for all the blessings you receive, this unleashes the power for you to receive even more than you already have. Generally, around Thanksgiving we officially enter into "peak gratitude season," when we celebrate our thankfulness for all the good things in our lives. Having the feeling of gratitude essentially means taking nothing for granted and giving thanks about the abundance in life that you have obtained.

Gratitude actually fits in with abundance in various aspects. Providing emphasis on a feeling of gratitude towards whatever life offers you immediately bring you into an energetic alignment having an increased abundance. Gratitude is what really keeps you stay connected to great power. As a famous writer says, "A lot of people are trapped in the state of poverty by having lack of gratitude." Abundance always goes with gratitude because we can always attract great wealth as well as abundance with the power of gratitude. Have you ever wondered why your life is not really abundant, why good things don't happen to you, why aren't you completely happy?

Is it because you are living in a life full of complaints like the majority? This is actually one of the main reasons behind your lack of abundance in life. If you always see things negatively, you will never appreciate the good things you possess and the blessing you receive. Ingratitude attracts scarcity. Why not change the way you see things? But wouldn't it be wonderful to experience that level of joy, love, and appreciation every day of the year? How would it change your life if you did? Start looking at everything in your life as a blessing and as good things to be grateful for, then your life will become meaningful and you will be happy. Your sense of gratitude will bring great abundance that you have been dreaming of. The way you see life, the way you think about the things around you, make a huge difference about how abundant you are in your life today.

The feeling of gratitude is really powerful and it an essential part of your life that has the ability to bring yourself to the things you want. When you start looking and focusing your own energy on being truly grateful, you bring real abundance in your life. Hence, never underestimate the power of gratitude. It is one of the highest emotional states you can experience. When you cultivate gratitude, you're able to feel true joy and contentment, no matter what you have or don't have in your life. The more grateful you are with what you have, the more you will attract more for which you can be grateful. Gratitude always fits in with abundance. They primary key towards obtaining real abundance in life is through learning to become grateful even in though you are living in an ungrateful world.

2) Getting In The Right Mindset

Having the right mindset means finding something to be grateful for in every difficulty. If you have the right way of thinking about life and the things around you, you are able to see the opportunity behind every problem. If you are able to acknowledge the good things in your life amidst diversity, you have the right mindset that will lead you towards a happy life.

In the face of difficulties and in today's sinking economy, it is really difficult for us to remain appreciative and grateful. Once you feel overwhelmed and stressed out, it is sometimes hard to find reasons to become grateful. It is true that most of the times, finding the good in difficult situation can really be challenging. However, the great benefits of maintaining appreciation and genuine gratitude in spite of what is going on around you, are truly worth looking into. Having the right mindset about being grateful and appreciative can greatly transform your life. You need to get the right mindset in order to unleash unlimited abundance in your life. Learn to Count your Blessings

Each of us has our own blessings in life. Regardless of who you are, where you came from, or what you are going through, you always have blessings in your life that you can be grateful for. The only challenge here is to educate yourself to provide emphasis on gratitude and search for many reasons in order for you to manifest appreciation. If you are a type of person who is not really appreciative, well this is the best time for you to develop your new habit. This habit is about searching for something to be thankful for about every situation, experience that you encounter or person. Why is it so important to be grateful?

Why do we need to cultivate this habit? All because we choose to train our attention on is what we consciously think about. So if we choose to focus on what we're grateful for, our overall feeling of well-being improves. We find the world to be a kinder place. You'll start to notice more things to appreciate. Your feeling of abundance just keeps growing and growing. Gratitude has many benefits in that it can keep you from feeling inadequate. It can keep your mind focused on the good rather than the bad. You can think more abundantly by having gratitude. This is why you must obey the Law of Gratitude if you want what you seek.

Think about this. If your show of gratitude is strong, the results that come back to you will be strong. If your debt of gratitude is continuous, your supply will also be continuous. If you start losing your attitude of gratitude, you will find you will loose ground rapidly and end up on the losing end of life. In every difficult situation that you encounter, this can really be difficult, but if you are able to develop this habit, you can see significant changes in your life and how you view life itself. You just have to work hard in finding a little piece of diamond in a huge rocky mountain.

You can also give thanks for a loving relationship with your partner and family, good health and those positive outcomes in various situations. Gratitude is really powerful and being fully aware of the blessings you receive can have huge impacts on your life. If you are filled with thankfulness and appreciation, this change your reality's dynamic. Genuinely express appreciation and gratitude for those people around you. If something good happen to you, no matter how big or small it is, be thankful that it happens. If you get into the right mindset about having a feeling of gratitude towards others and each situation, you will also feel good about yourself. You will have a different perspective about life and you will view the world as something beautiful.

It is truly amazing how a positive action can create so much change in the life of a person. Acknowledging the great power of attitude is actually one of the most important things today that create a great effect on one's life. In very tangible ways, it is true that gratitude is the key that opens the gateway to abundance.

3) List Down The Things You Are Grateful For

There are a lot of things around us to be grateful for; it's just a matter of appreciating the blessings you receive and acknowledging how blessed you for having them. Educating yourself for the feeling of attitude actually means taking nothing for granted and giving value to whatever you possess. Practice the attitude of never putting off an action or the word for the expression of your gratitude. Many individuals tend to take for granted the things that are present in their lives. There is actually a gratitude exercise instructing us to imagine losing few of the things that you are taking for granted today such as your family, your home, as well as your ability to hear and see, to walk or just anything that is currently giving you comfort.

Imagine losing them and then imagine that you are getting each of them back every day. Think how thankful you would be when it happens and when each one is given back to you. Starting finding happiness even in those small things you posses rather than holding out for great and big achievements like getting job promotion, having a baby or getting married. There are a lot of things to be grateful for. When you wake in the morning, be thankful for the life you have for another day. Your happiness always depends on how you view life itself and how you see your life today. If you begin to think that there are many more things to be grateful for, you will see how happy your life will be.

Use gratitude in order to guide you in putting things in their right perspective. If everything around you seems wrong, and if things do not go the way you want them to be, bear in mind that in every problem and difficulty carries the seeds of a greater benefit. When you are facing any challenge in your life and when you are in the face of great adversity, just ask yourself about the good things that you can get from it. Understand how you can benefit from a certain situation. Take some time today, wherever you are and whatever you're doing, to come up with a gratitude list. List everything you are thankful for to help you get through those slightly cloudy or downright stormy days when it's hard to conjure up a pile of thankfulness.

Like anything, gratitude is a learned behavior. It's something you find easier the more and more we you practice. If it doesn't come naturally, don't let that stop you from still giving thanks. There is still much to be thankful for, if we only have eyes to see. You can even be grateful for the littlest things that you probably never pay much attention to. These could be the simple things you can be grateful for even when times are tough...

You can feel gratitude for ...

1. Family, whether "by blood" or the people you've met in your life, that always make you feel at home
2. Your many significant others who are your true friends, who make life a lot easier to go through, and who love you more than you deserve
3. Good health if you have it, one of life's greatest pleasures. For any good health at all.
4. A roof over my head and a warm home
5. I am thankful for living in a town full of creative minds and opportunities
6. For a body that allows you to function in any way
7. For a brain that allows you to think about the world and its people in all the ways that you can
8. For access to water, one of life's most important necessities
9. For all the colors of the world that make life so much brighter than it would be otherwise.
10. For a phone that allows you to communicate with people instantaneously even when you are far away from them.
11. For good times and bad times – that we celebrate them or made it through them.
12. For faith, hope, and love. Because those things are free, irreplaceable, and the only things that last a lifetime.
13. The kindness of people I have never met before. The setbacks that have formed me and made me stronger.
14. For life, because without it none of the above is possible.

Use this list as a starting point and add any specifics you have. It's a good idea to pop the list on the fridge, or somewhere you can see it to remind yourself to be thankful throughout the day. Soon it will be second nature and you'll start to attract more good things to be thankful for.

4) Gratitude In Tough Times

Being grateful for bad things that happen to us isn't saying that what happened should have happened. It's not about lying down like a doormat; ready for the next punch life might throw at us. So we've covered all the good bits of our life and we're focusing on them. But what about the bad things that happen? Should we be grateful for them as well? Well yes, if possible. Being grateful about the bad things that happen is more about learning to live with the life you've had, and seeing the good that can spring from anything. When times are tough, or if you are in the midst of despair, or emotional mayhem, taking a moment to foster gratitude will create a sense of encouragement and calm when you need it most.

It is the last thing we can think of.

When we are facing difficulties, all we do is complain and ask why bad things are happening to us. Turning bad days into gratitude days is really a great challenge for many people, but it is always possible. Being grateful for hardship. This doesn't mean that the universe is going to give you more if it. It's more of a letting go. You can have two people in life experience exactly the same turn of unfortunate events and manage it completely differently. The person who uses gratitude that they are still alive, still surviving, still fighting, and has learnt from the lessons life has thrown upon them either at their own hand or at the hand of others is the one who is going to be positively affected by having gratitude in their life.

Learn to count your blessings, not your problems. Gratitude can help you cope with hard times... People spend most of their time lamenting about their problems, complaining about the difficulties they suffer from that they no longer care about the blessings that they have received. When faced in difficulties, people really tend to forget what they have and the good things in their life. Don't get me wrong. I am not suggesting that gratitude will come easily or naturally in a crisis. It's easy to feel grateful for the good things. No one "feels" grateful that he or she got into an accident or lost her new watch or credit card.

But it is vital to make a distinction between *feeling* grateful and *being* grateful. We don't have total control over our emotions. We cannot easily control ourselves to feel grateful, less depressed, or happy. Feelings follow from the way we look at the world, thoughts we have about the way things are, the way things should be, and the distance between these two points. Hence, it is important to practice to count your blessings during tough times. Learn to look at the brighter side of every situation. If you experience problems and difficulties at work, be more grateful that you have your own work. If you are facing challenges in life, be more grateful of these challenges because due to them, your life is not boring. If you are facing trials in your life today, be thankful that these can give you much strength to overcome more trials in the future. Appreciate your challenges in life that can help you learn and be a stronger person.

To say that we are grateful does not mean that everything in your life is perfect; it only means that you are aware of all your blessings in spite of the challenges that you are experiencing. If you remain angry, upset and frustrated because you are having a really bad day, that won't change anything. In fact, that would make things worse. Being grateful during these times can brighten up your day as well as others. Getting what you want is not the only reason for you to grateful, sometimes, your appreciation in life becomes even more valuable when you learn to be appreciative in times of troubles and difficulties.

If you are in a difficult situation, instead of hating the world for giving you such problem, think of the benefit that you can benefit from it. Think about the things that you can gain from this situation and through this, you will become more inspired to overcome the difficult situation you are into. Always look for something to be grateful for in every bad day you face. Also, it is better to understand the reason you are in such situation and think of the best things that you can obtain from it. If you learn to become more grateful and happy with every situation you are in, you can become happier in your life. Always be grateful that you do not already have all the things that you want because if you did, there will be nothing more to look forward to. Be more grateful for every difficult situation you are into because in those times, you are able to grow.

5) How Gratitude Can Change What you Attract

Being grateful in any kind of situation is really a powerful and strong attracting force. Gratitude reduces negativity, helps people learn, improves relationships and most importantly, gratitude attracts that things that you want. This is a great and powerful force that can change what one is able to attract. Having gratitude helps us to enjoy life more. It can break through huge barriers and reduce our stress loads, give us more confidence and help us to meet our goals- no matter how big they may be.

Once you find things you appreciate and you start providing emphasis on the things you are thankful for, you can always attract them. As you start flooding your mind with gratitude or appreciation, you actually attract more of those that you want. If you are in a state of gratitude, you are also in a high energy vibration essential in attracting more things that you can be thankful for. There will also be more things that will magically come to you – things that are actually drawn into you by your focus and great feelings of gratitude.

Getting What You Want Gratitude brings you more of what you appreciate. 106 Every time you flood your mind with appreciation or gratitude you attract more of what you desire.

Why?

Because providing more focus on the things that you really want in life and thus, you are attracting more of these things into your own life. When you are grateful, you're in a high energy vibration that will attract more things to be grateful for and more good things will come to you magically, drawn in by your feelings of gratitude. The emotion of joy attracts conditions of joy. This is why it is important to keep a gratitude list so you know what to focus on.

Also, gratitude makes the things that you want more tangible and serves as real aspect of your reality. The more real and tangible your desires are, the more you will provide great focus on them. As being said, gratitude is really powerful. It can resolve problems, improves your life, helps you learn and attract the things that you want. This can greatly change what you attract because the more aware you are about the blessings and good things you receive, you give more Take time each day to express your gratitude for all of the good things in your life and you will soon begin to experience the benefits. focus to it by expressing your appreciation. This will in turn enable you to attract positive energies to obtain what you want.

Gratitude really matters. It does not only allow us to obtain what we want but it also leads to positive actions. When one feels grateful for the kindness showed by a person, one may be more likely to show kindness in the person in return. This is then really helpful in creating good relationships with others. With many blessings that you can take benefit from appreciation and giving thanks on the things you receive, there is no reason for you not to the practice the attitude of gratitude. This will not only attract good things on your life but on the lives of others as well.